```
J                    567430
362.88               11.95
McG
McGuire
Victims
```

DATE DUE			

GREAT RIVER REGIONAL LIBRARY

St. Cloud, Minnesota 56301

Women Today

Victims

by
Leslie McGuire

The Rourke Corporation, Inc.
Vero Beach, Florida 32964

Copyright 1991 by The Rourke Corporation, Inc.

All rights reserved. No part of this book may be reproduced or utilized in any form or by any means, electronic or mechanical, including photocopying, recording or by any information storage and retrieval system without permission in writing from the publisher.

The Rourke Corporation, Inc.
P.O. Box 3328, Vero Beach, FL 32964

McGuire, Leslie.
   Victims / by Leslie McGuire.
      p. cm. —(Women today)
   Includes bibliographical references and index.
   Summary: Examines rape and other types of violent attacks on women and discusses their possible causes, effects, and means of prevention.
   ISBN 0-86593-120-8
   1. Women—United States—Crimes against—Juvenile literature. 2. Rape victims—United States—Juvenile literature. 3. Abused women—United States—Juvenile literature. [1. Rape. 2. Violence.] I. Title. II. Series.
HV6250.4.W65M34   1991
362.88'082—dc20   91-11041
                                                                                       CIP
                                                                                        AC

Series Editor: Elizabeth Sirimarco
Editors: Gregory Lee, Marguerite Aronowitz
Book design and production: The Creative Spark, Capistrano Beach, California
Cover Photograph: Edward Lettau/Photo Researchers, Inc.

Contents

	Introduction	4
1.	The Reality Of Violence	6
2.	Social And Emotional Forces	14
3.	What Is Abuse?	22
4.	Rape	32
5.	Leaving A Bad Situation	42
6.	A Woman's Rights	52
	Glossary	60
	Bibliography	62
	Index	63

Introduction

Throughout history, a number of cultures have respected and valued women—even worshipped motherhood. But it was and is a nearly universal assumption that women are "the weaker sex." Biologically, the human male is generally stronger and can force his will upon most females. While women usually live longer lives, the tradeoff seems to be in their physical and cultural domination by men. Unfortunately, this means that women suffer more often from violent crimes related in some way to their gender—for example, rape, sexual exploitation, and battering.

In recent times, society has begun to recognize the alarming amount of physical and emotional violence to which women are subjected. In our society, with its many freedoms, there are people who take advantage of others. They go beyond law and morality to inflict pain and emotional abuse on those who cannot defend themselves. Because of this, many abused children grow up to be abusive adults, and many battered women were abused as children.

Women in our society experience forms of violence just because they are women. These problems deserve special attention and education. In this book we will discuss frankly some of the ways women are victimized, why it happens, and what they can do about it.

1 The Reality Of Violence

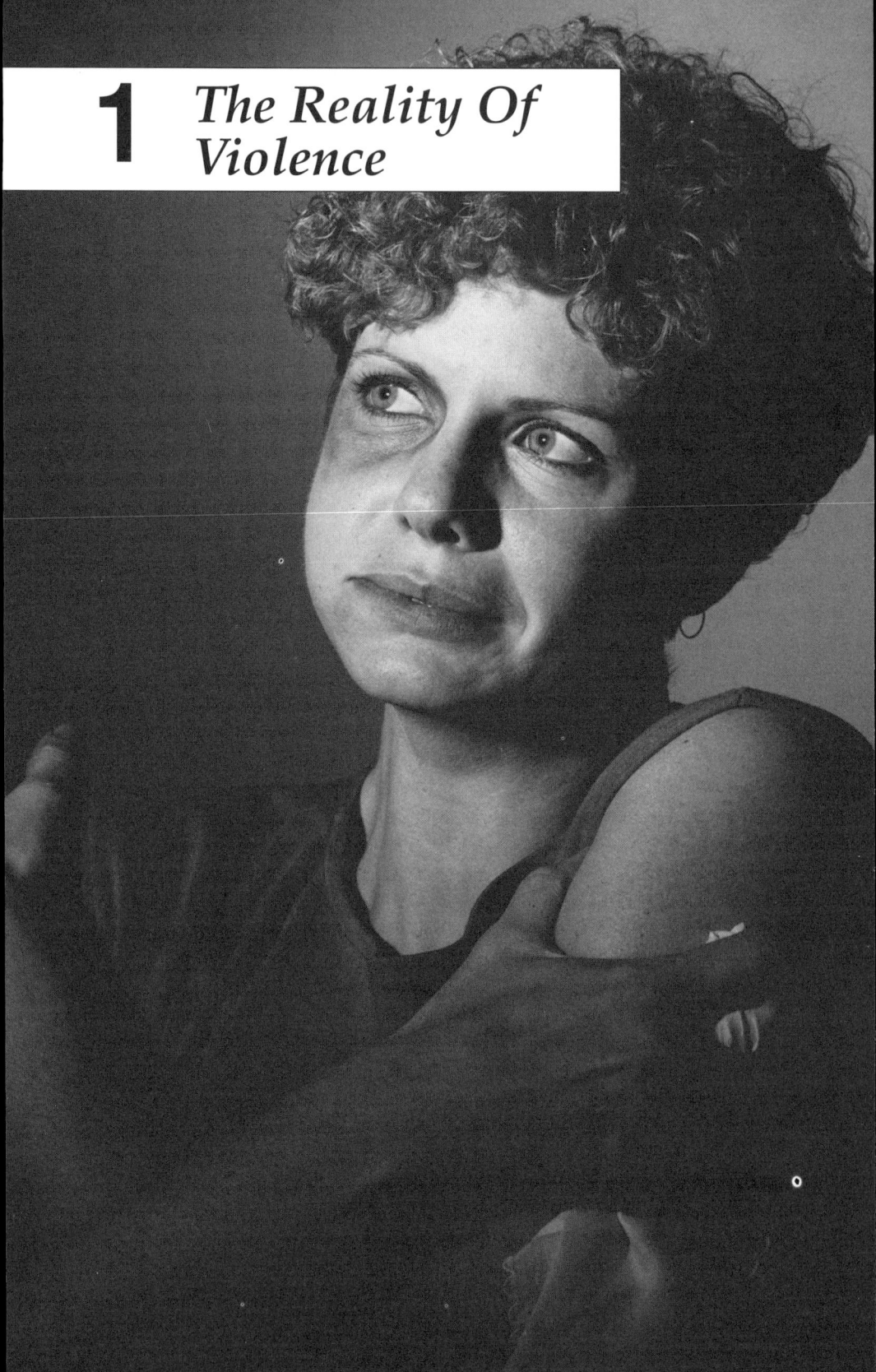

Ginny had just started her first year of college. She was away from home for the first time in her life, and she was enjoying her new independence. She and a friend went to a party in one of the fraternity houses. Ginny met a handsome student she had seen in one of her classes. Carl spent the evening talking with her, flattering her, and telling her how glad he was to have finally met a girl with "real brains."

He offered to take her back to her dorm after the party. Ginny was thrilled. But after driving down a deserted road, Carl stopped the car and began to aggressively kiss Ginny. At first she was flattered, but when he started putting his hands under her shirt, Ginny became angry. When she refused to have sex with him, Carl threatened to throw her out of the car.

"He told me I could walk home by myself. But it was one o'clock in the morning, and I had no idea where I was. It was freezing out there. I asked him to just please take me home. After that, he raped me. It was as if he figured it was the price I should pay for the ride."

Ginny was a victim of *date rape*: Her attacker was someone she had met, and also someone she had liked. Ginny is a fine young woman who goes to a good school. Her attacker seemed like a "nice" young man.

Charlotte And Laura

Charlotte ran away from home when she was 15. She had been sexually abused by her father from the time she was six years old, and he had threatened to kill her if she told anyone. Her mother probably knew what was happening, but either couldn't or wouldn't do anything to stop it. Finally Charlotte decided that life on the street would be better than life at home.

Laura was in a similar situation. However, instead of running away, she told her boyfriend about her father. The boyfriend was furious. Encouraged by Laura's anger, he and a couple of his friends tried to kill her father. Their attempt failed. The two boys were brought up on assault charges, convicted, and are now serving time in jail. Laura was tried as an accessory. Because she is a minor, she is now on probation.

Both Charlotte and Laura were victims of *sexual abuse*. And yet the way they responded to that abuse didn't make their lives any better. But they felt they had no other choice, no other way to handle what appeared to be an impossible situation.

Jeanette

After graduating from high school, Jeanette got her first job in a textile factory. She was a receptionist in the sales office. About a month after she started working, her boss started asking her to work late. Jeanette wanted very much to do a good job. She was hoping for a raise, so she wanted to impress the man who hired her.

As the weeks went by, it became clear that her boss expected her to do more than work. He wanted her to have sex with him. Besides propositioning her when they were alone, he put his hands on her while threatening to fire her if she told anyone. Jeanette was afraid of being fired so quickly after she had started her first job, so she put up with his behavior. But as time went by, she became more and more uncomfortable. Her boss was married, and even had children. One day after hours he tried to force her to have sexual intercourse with him. Jeanette quit.

Jeanette was a victim of *sexual harassment*, something that can happen anywhere—at school or on the job. It is not uncommon, and is against the law. Yet many women feel that it's their fault. If a woman complains, her boss may say that she's not doing her job well, and that this is her way of getting back at him for criticizing her work. People often believe the boss, instead of the employee, since the boss has more power in the company.

Women in both blue-collar and white-collar professions can experience stress on the job due to sexual harassment in the workplace.

Sex Or Violence?

When a man forces a woman to have intercourse with him, it is not a sexual act. It is a mistake to think a rapist forces himself upon a female because he is attracted to her. In fact, rape is an act of power or aggression—it is physical assault. When a male wants to prove his power over a female in this way, he is usually only trying to prove it to himself or take revenge on females in general.

The statistics on both reported and unreported sexual violence show that one in three girls and one in ten boys will be the targets of sexual abuse before they are age 18. In a recent poll, one in 12 young men admitted committing acts that met the legal definition of rape. But only one percent of them saw their behavior as criminal.

One study of campus date rape showed that one in nine female students had been raped; eight out of ten of these women knew the person who did it. A 1988 survey showed that four out of five campus rapes were committed by students. The most upsetting thing about the survey, however, was that only five percent of the young women who were raped reported it.

Domestic Violence

One day in November 1987, a distraught woman in New York City made a 911 call and said her daughter had choked on a piece of food and was not breathing right. When police arrived at the expensive Greenwich Village apartment, they didn't find the choking problem they'd expected. The little girl's mother, Hedda Nussbaum, took them to the room where her adopted daughter, Elizabeth, lay. The six-year-old was badly bruised and breathing with difficulty. Her little brother was tied with string to his playpen. He was filthy, clothed only in soaked diapers. And Hedda had been beaten as well.

Little Elizabeth died a week later from wounds she

had sustained in the beating. This violence had been only the latest in the abuse she'd suffered for most of her life. Her guardians, Hedda Nussbaum and Joel Steinberg, a prominent New York criminal lawyer, were arrested for murder.

Hedda Nussbaum was both well-off and educated. So was the man she lived with, 46-year-old Steinberg. The newspapers were filled with pictures of Hedda's face ravaged from beatings she had received at the hands of Steinberg. She was seen as the classic "battered wife." But this couple didn't fit the picture that most people have of battered women and abused children.

Many Americans think family or *domestic* violence only occurs in poor or minority families, or in households where alcohol and drugs are used regularly. But society is learning that violence in families occurs more often than anyone had believed. It can affect any family, regardless of their economic, social or educational background. There is no single profile of a violent family, a battered wife, or an abused child.

In most cases of rape and domestic violence, the victims are women and children. Sometimes men or old people are abused. Usually the victim doesn't want to talk about what happened. Family violence, rape, sexual abuse, and sexual harassment were considered, until recently, to be *taboo* subjects—ones you don't talk about. The reason seems to be that if no one talks about it, it must not exist or it will disappear all by itself.

Violence In History

Violence against women and children is an age-old problem that has its roots in inequality. Since early times, most cultures have been dominated by men. Women and children were considered to be their personal property. The resulting belief has been that a man can do whatever he wants with his personal property—even destroy it.

In ancient Rome, for example, a father could decide

This eighth-grade sex education teacher includes a lecture on rape and sexual abuse—two subjects that used to be taboo in public school classrooms. Early education is an important tool in preventing the victimization of women.

whether his disobedient children would live or die, and who they would marry. He could have an adulterous wife put to death. In the Middle Ages the law stated that the husband was the head of the household. The woman and man together had only one identity—that of the husband.

English law allowed men to physically punish wives and children. The "rule of thumb" is an expression taken from English law that says a husband may beat his wife with a rod that is not "thicker than his thumb." The Puritans even had the "right" to put their unmanageable children to death.

In the United States, before the Civil War, wives could not own property even if they inherited it. If they were married, their inheritance went to the husbands. Husbands could also take any money their wives earned. Women had many responsibilities, but few rights under the law.

Although laws have been passed during the 20th century to protect women, patterns of behavior are often difficult to change. Females are still thought of by many males as objects to be used or threatened with physical violence. Many social and emotional causes that contribute to the continuing violence against women are just excuses that should be recognized as such and brought under control. For example, most men who commit violent acts do not think of themselves as violent. Instead, they say that sometimes they "just can't control their anger." This excuse is often accepted by our culture.

There are also many side effects of violence that people don't always recognize, like the fact that children who come from homes that are violent often become violent parents themselves. It is important to try to stop violence within the family, because unless we do, there is little chance we will be able to heal the suffering that occurs as a result of violence—both in our own society and all over the world.

2 Social And Emotional Forces

In legal terms, there is a lot of confusion between the definition of "sex" and "rape." If a female doesn't agree to have sex with a male but is forced to give in, the act is rape. In many states, however, in order to prove it was rape, there has to be strong evidence that the victim fought back. In New York, for example, there is the "bite, kick, scratch and scream" definition. If a woman doesn't fight back in a way that leaves visible marks on her body, it is difficult to prove that she didn't consent to have sex. Even though weapons and threats of violence may be used by the male, a court may still think that the rape was the woman's fault.

Jane

Jane was on her way home from work about nine o'clock on a very cold night. No one else was out. She lived in a middle-class neighborhood where there had never been any news of people getting mugged or having purses stolen.

"As I got close to my house," says Jane, "a man suddenly jumped up from between two cars. He grabbed my arm and asked for a cigarette. I told him to let go of me and that I didn't have any."

Jane remembered she had been told not to startle a potential attacker. She thought of screaming, but was afraid that the man might turn violent. So she tried to act cool, as if there were nothing to be afraid of. She turned to walk away, but he grabbed her again and pushed her down on the ground between two parked cars.

"As he pushed me down, he started whispering," said Jane. "He said he had already killed three people, and if I screamed or did anything he would kill me, too. I didn't see a weapon, but I was too terrified to do anything."

After she was raped, she asked him if she could get up. He laughed at her, and she remembered that rapists sometimes killed their victims anyway. She simply waited, quietly, until he ran off.

The Reasons

Women's rights activists have argued that if a woman is threatened with rape, she may be so frightened that her terror will prevent her from doing anything at all. Her attacker is often physically larger, clearly violent, and may well have a weapon. A woman may not fight back in order to save her life. Or she may simply be frozen with fear.

Sometimes opinions differ about what is a "real rape." Some say that men are naturally aggressive and have trouble controlling their sexual urges. With this kind of philosophy, women who are attractive, alone, or dressed in revealing clothing are "asking for it." In those instances, some people feel that men are simply acting on their instincts. They refuse to acknowledge that rape is violence against females, not normal male behavior. The only cases taken seriously are those in which the stereotypical rapist is seen as a sexual *pervert* who hides in the bushes and stalks his victim. Statistics tell us, however, that a lot more women are raped than we ever imagined. And one of the most frightening statistics is that most women are raped by people they already know.

The typical rapist is most often an ordinary man, with an ordinary background, not a "criminal type." This explains why some people believe that it is the woman's behavior that causes rape. So if the majority of rapists are ordinary men who are not to be blamed, is society in part responsible for violence against women? Is rape just another form of acceptable behavior in our culture—when women are forced to have sex as part of the "normal" interaction between men and women?

The leader of the Rape Awareness Program at Southern Methodist University says, "The entire American dating system is basically oriented toward wearing down a woman's resistance until she finally gives in. We need to make them (men) understand that when a woman says 'no,' she means no."

No matter how "normal" a boy seems, or how safe you may feel on a date, it is important to remember that not all rapists are "criminal types."

This, then, means that sexual intercourse is only okay if both parties agree to participate. No matter what society says, a female doesn't have to give in to sex if she doesn't want to. And she doesn't have to bow to the wishes of a male just because he may be physically stronger, or threaten violence.

There are many reasons for violence against women. Women as a group are physically weaker than men. They are also socially weaker. Despite changes in society since the women's movement, men still have more power than women in our society. Men are paid more. Men also have more authority in the workplace. Women often must take care of their children. This leaves them less time to pursue a career or other personal interests that men generally take for granted. Although women in the United States have more rights and opportunities today than ever before, things are far from being equal between the sexes.

Has the women's movement helped change our culture in ways that are difficult for men to deal with? After all, the man's traditional role has been as provider and head of the household. As more women enter the work force and compete for jobs, men may fear loss of power and control. This fear may lead to anger directed at women, and take the form of violence.

Some researchers believe that men who feel inferior to their wives or to women in general believe they have no other outlet but to attack them with a show of physical force. One common profile of an abusive husband is one whose wife has a better job or makes more money than he does. But this is not always the case.

In the 1960s the United States Commission on the Causes and Prevention of Violence found that one out of four men and one out of six women said they felt there were circumstances where it would be all right for a husband to hit his wife. Seven out of ten people thought it was good if a boy has a few fistfights as he

In families where parents share the job of raising children, and respect everyone's rights, the frequency of domestic violence is lessened.

grows up. This seems to indicate that there is not only some public acceptance of violence from men, but that people seem to encourage it.

Private Abuse

As cities and suburbs become more and more crowded, many people develop strong urges to maintain their privacy. It's harder to make friends with their neighbors. And our society is more on the go than ever before, separating families far and wide. Could this modern trend toward isolation and privacy in the family encourage a climate of family violence? Each family lives on its own, with fewer household members than in the past. Single-parent families are much more common. In the past, when many people lived in *extended families*, children and often relatives witnessed violence that took place within the family. There were fewer places where a violent person could hide his or her behavior. Today, when neighbors don't interfere and relatives aren't around to see what's happening, everyone tries hard to protect the image of being the "perfect family"—including the abuser and the abused.

Another cause of family violence—aside from economic and physical inequality between men and women and the added factor of greater privacy—is the fact that people *can* be violent.

When Bob is at the office, he has to deal with difficult people all day long. His boss criticizes him unfairly. The maintenance man accidentally knocks a lamp off his desk and breaks it. His secretary sends a letter in the wrong envelope. And one of his biggest accounts decides to change companies. Bob could vent his anger by hitting his boss in the mouth or slapping his secretary. But if he were to do this, in all likelihood, he would face assault charges. They would file a complaint with the police or someone higher up in the company, and Bob would be in a lot of trouble.

When Bob is home, however, if his wife cooks a

dinner he doesn't like, or his three-year-old breaks the VCR, he can vent his anger on them without having to worry about going to jail.

In domestic disputes, if the police are called, they often encourage the husband and wife to "kiss and make up." If a child is hit or beaten, unless they are seriously injured, usually no one ever finds out about it. Even in cases where serious injury does occur, authorities can be very slow to step in. For example, in the case of little Elizabeth Steinberg, neighbors said they had reported the abuse over and over again to police and social agencies. But nothing was ever done until it was too late.

People abuse family members because they are easy targets. And violence makes a person feel powerful. If children are doing things that are annoying, hitting them usually makes them stop. If a wife makes a husband feel weak or stupid, or if she criticizes him, hitting her shows her who the real power is in the family. Violent people get an immediate feeling of gratification that makes them feel powerful and in control.

If appropriate punishment for domestic violence and human abuse is so hard to find, and if violence is glorified all around us, is it any wonder that violence in the family is close to being epidemic?

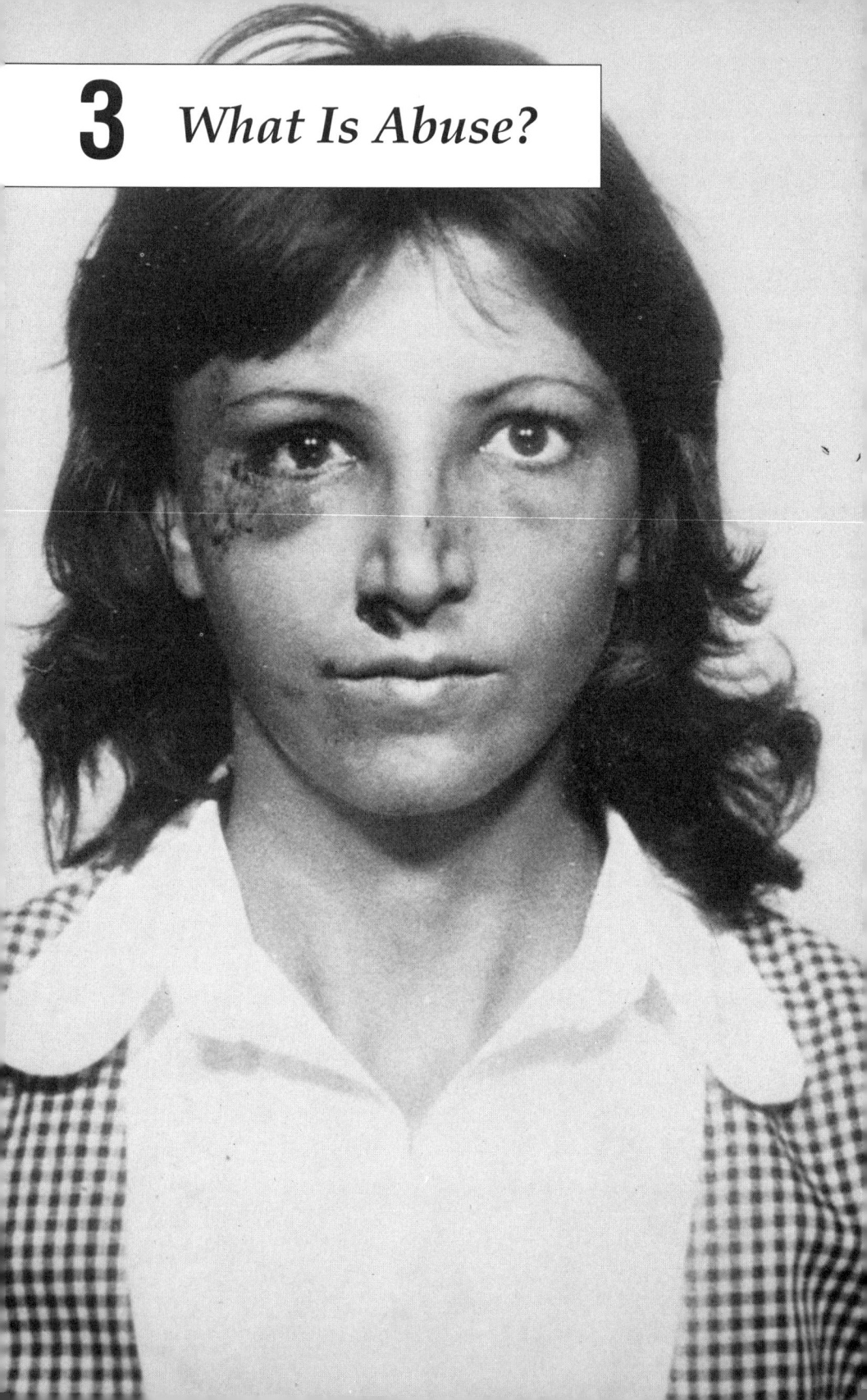

3 What Is Abuse?

Being abused by someone who is close to you is a very frightening and lonely experience. Many women and girls aren't even sure that they are being abused. So it is important to know what abuse is.

Abuse for a female in an intimate relationship is when the partner—a husband or boyfriend—repeatedly causes physical or emotional harm. Abusive behavior can take many forms: pushing, hitting, punching, beating, pinching, slapping, shaking, biting, pulling hair, stabbing, throwing objects, driving recklessly, using humiliating language, forcing sex, and denying proper medical care when ill or pregnant.

Women are also considered to be victimized if they are threatened, continually accused of having affairs or flirting, humiliated in public, called names, criticized constantly, or have their feelings and thoughts ignored or belittled.

Studies show that if a male ever physically abuses his partner more than once, he will probably continue to abuse her. And usually the abuse gets worse, not better. As soon as he sees that this kind of behavior is tolerated, he will continue to do it.

A woman continues to be a victim if the physical abuse has stopped, but her partner emotionally abuses her by threatening her. If she has lost her ability to make decisions regarding her own welfare, she is still being abused. A woman is considered to be a victim even if she is not married to her partner, or if she has ended the relationship but her ex-partner is still abusive.

A good way to determine whether or not a woman is being abused is to ask questions. Is she afraid of her partner? Is she afraid of her partner's reaction if she expresses an opinion? Does she have to ask for permission to visit friends or relatives? Is she always trying to make everything "perfect?" Does she try to please her partner all the time, only to be criticized again? Does she feel that her partner has two different personalities? Is she beginning to believe all the bad things her partner says about her? Is she afraid to leave him? If the answer to any of these questions is yes, then there is a good chance that the female in question is in an abusive relationship.

A Vicious Cycle: Child Abuse

Many times the reason a woman accepts this kind of physical or emotional abuse is because she was abused as a child. She sees this kind of hurting as an acceptable part of family life, perhaps just another way of behaving when you love someone.

Young children who are abused are powerless to do anything about it. They rarely think their parents are bad or crazy. They cannot leave, and they cannot demand better treatment. Children often do not even realize that they are being abused. They may think that all young people are treated the same way. They learn to accept the abuse, and may even think it is their own fault.

Child abuse can take many different forms. *Neglect* is when a parent doesn't provide enough food, clothing, medical attention or shelter. For example, leaving children alone when they are unable to care for themselves is neglect. It leaves them in a dangerous situation.

Emotional neglect occurs when parents don't take an interest in their children. The children feel unwanted and unloved. Alcoholic parents are often neglectful, and even though this form of neglect doesn't leave physical scars, it often has very serious consequences when the children grow up.

Children can also be psychologically abused by a parent. If a parent calls them names, makes them feel stupid, or humiliates them, it is abusive behavior. Parents can threaten to abandon their children or throw them out of the house. They can also threaten them with physical violence or other forms of punishment like, "I'm going to call the police and have them put you in jail."

Physical abuse occurs when children are whipped, beaten, pinched, pushed, slapped or burned. Some of this damage will be visible, but some of the injuries can be internal, such as hemorrhaging, or broken bones.

Punishment resulting in physical injuries is certainly abuse. Even spanking can be abuse—especially if it is severe and out of control. Using objects to hit a child, or a closed fist, or hitting children in delicate parts of their bodies—such as the head, stomach, back or genitals, is abuse. Cruel and inhuman punishment such as locking a child in the closet or forcing him or her to do something that is too difficult for the child's age or ability are also considered to be child abuse.

Sexual abuse is when any person, adult or child, forces or tricks someone into having any kind of unwanted sexual contact. Showing children X-rated pictures or movies, or describing sexual acts, is a form of sexual abuse. Touching their genitals is a serious form of sexual abuse that is called *molestation.*

This severe kind of punishment or abuse is a result of lack of respect for children and their rights. If children are brought up to feel they have no rights at all when faced with an authority figure, it is perfectly natural for them to feel they have no rights as adults, either. When children are abused, they feel powerless. Sometimes they react by wanting to be just like their abuser, because they also want to have that power. After all, they will need power to protect themselves. So when they grow up, sometimes they will also become abusers, getting their revenge on their own children. And so the dangerous cycle continues unbroken.

Many adults who were abused as children find themselves in abusive relationships when they are grown. For example, when Marybeth was little, her father spanked her regularly. Many times it was for things she had done accidentally. Often she was locked in her room for long periods of time.

"The worst part of it," says Marybeth, "was that

National Rally for Equal Rights

The women's movement of the late 1960s and '70s helped focus attention on the plight of women in many areas of our society.

sometimes I really had to go to the bathroom. But I had to hold it in until they let me out of my room. It was so painful, sometimes it was worse than the beating."

But Marybeth's father also told her how much he loved her, how pretty she was, and how glad he was to have such a beautiful little girl. Marybeth was constantly confused. Was she good, or was she bad? Clearly, her father loved her, because he said so. When he punished her it had to be because he loved her and didn't like it when she did certain things. She believed all the beatings were her own fault.

When Marybeth grew up and met John, she thought she was the luckiest girl alive. He was handsome, had a good job, and seemed to love her very much.

"I knew that he loved me a lot because he was so jealous," said Marybeth. "He got real upset when I talked to other boys. He once told me he would kill me if he ever caught me with anyone else. He didn't believe me when I said I was going out with my girlfriends. Soon, I only saw him, and I really didn't mind a bit. It was because I knew he loved me, and I didn't want to hurt him."

John started cutting Marybeth off from her friends. About a year after they were married, he started hitting her. Marybeth had just given birth, and she thought the baby made John jumpy. She waited for him to adjust to the added responsibility, but the beatings continued.

"I suppose I could have left him," said Marybeth. "But how could I? I had a small child. I had never had a real job in my life. I couldn't support us, and I couldn't go home, either. My parents would have been so angry at me. My mother was always telling me that marriage is hard, and sometimes you just have to put up with things that you don't like and try to please your man."

Soon Marybeth started to feel as if everything were her fault. John told her that the house was never clean enough, and the meals didn't taste good enough. She believed she wasn't sexy, pretty or smart enough.

"I felt I was lucky to have as good a husband as I did," she said. "After all, who else would want me? Certainly not someone as handsome and successful as John."

Myths

The following are some myths about abuse:

MYTH: If a person stays in an abusive relationship, it is because they are "asking" to be abused.

FACT: Nobody wants to be abused. When a woman stays in an abusive relationship, it is not because she likes it. She is probably afraid to leave for a number of reasons. Probably her partner threatens her. If she has children he probably threatens to take them away from her if she leaves. She may be afraid that she cannot support herself and her children without her spouse. She may think that all men act this way, and that another relationship would be no different. Perhaps she stays for religious reasons, or because she doesn't want her children to be without a father. Most of the time she is terrified of what will happen to her if she tries to break away.

MYTH: Only low-income or minority women are abused.
FACT: Women of all ages, races, economic and educational backgrounds can find themselves in abusive relationships. Some studies have shown that abuse often happens to women in high-income brackets. Often these women are too embarrassed to ask for help because of their social standing. If they do, they go to private sources like friends or relatives, so as few people as possible will find out about it. On the other hand, lower income women often have to ask for public assistance, so there is more documented evidence of their cases.

MYTH: Alcohol and drug abuse cause physical abuse.
FACT: Even though there is a close relationship between extreme drug and alcohol use and abusive behavior, they are excuses, not the cause. Studies have shown that 25 percent of abusive partners do not use alcohol at all. And drugs have an even smaller connection with abuse of women. It is important for females to know that eliminating drug or alcohol use, or getting counseling for drugs or alcohol abuse, will not necessarily make the physical or emotional abuse stop.

MYTH: Men who abuse their partners are mentally ill.
FACT: Only a small percentage of the abusers can be labeled as mentally ill, but many people want to believe this myth. It makes them feel better to believe that men who abuse women are "sick." Few people want to deal with such a private problem as domestic violence and abuse of women. Claiming that wife beaters are sick allows people to ignore cultural attitudes that have encouraged men to abuse their partners for centuries.

MYTH: Abusing one's partner in private doesn't really have any effect on the children.
FACT: Even if children never see the abuse, they will suspect it because of their mother's high degree of stress. Children in shelters, even young ones, are aware of violence. When someone is physically violent with a woman who is a mother, they abuse her children emotionally. And in families where the mother is abused, the children are often victims of physical abuse as well. When they finally grow up and become parents, they often model themselves after their own parents. Thus children who grow up in violent households are at risk of becoming violent adults.

Many abused women will deny that they are abused. They lie to doctors, friends and family members. They may tell police officers or others who have tried to help them to "go away," that "everything is fine now." They may make excuses for their partner's behavior by saying, "He's really a wonderful husband," or "It was my fault."

A nagging problem regarding abuse is society's tendency to see the victim as the cause. Abused women are often asked, "What did you do?" It is the same as suggesting that a woman wanted to be raped by asking, "Did you enjoy it?"

Many battered women feel guilt and shame about the abuse they take. As Marybeth said, "I didn't want to admit that such a thing was going on in my house. I felt

Many women do not know where to turn if they are in an abusive household. Fortunately, there are shelters for battered women and their children in most cities where they can seek counseling, help, and temporary housing.

dirty and ashamed. John was such a perfect husband on the outside. I thought everyone would blame me. It took a long time for me to finally face what was happening and ask for help. That's when I discovered that someone would actually help me, not blame me."

Women need to face the truth if they are being victimized and want it to end. The only way to change the way abusive people behave is to show them that what they're doing is wrong. If no one admits that something bad is happening, they cannot begin to change it for themselves or for future generations.

4 *Rape*

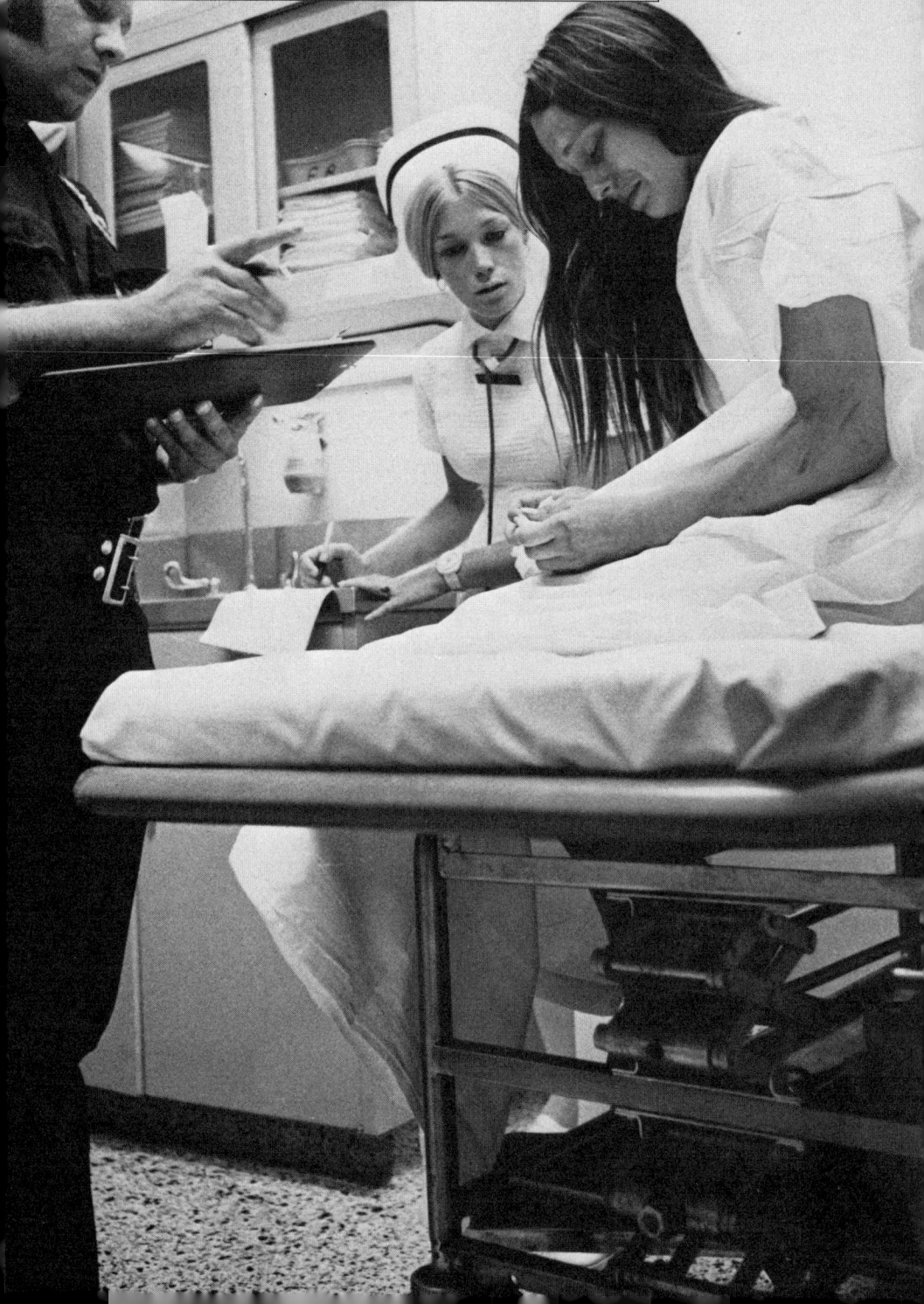

School years are supposed to be a wonderful time. There are so many things to learn about, so many new friends to make. Young women prepare themselves for a whole new life as adults. They form opinions, develop interesting lifestyles, and are constantly growing and moving forward. But sometimes things happen that burst the bubble of youth and create havoc in a young life.

One night in 1988 Eleanor was raped. She still has trouble talking about it. Two years later the last of her attackers was prosecuted, but she still can't forget what happened. Eleanor had been drinking, and so were the young men involved. This is typical of date rape cases—50 percent of the females and 75 percent of the males have been drinking before such assaults take place. In fact, many young men try to use alcohol to weaken a young woman's determination not to have sex.

Eleanor had been drinking by herself to try to calm her nerves. She was both excited and scared at the prospect of her date with a 23-year-old fraternity member. Eleanor was just a first-year college student. When she got to the fraternity house, her date, Daniel, took her to his room and gave her a bottle of wine. He told her to finish it off. Later tests would put her blood alcohol level at about .349, which is enough to cause death.

Eleanor doesn't remember what happened to her next, but her date returned, forced her to have sex with him, then carried her to the shower room. There, at least two of his fraternity brothers forced her to have sex with them. When police found her later, she was unconscious, bleeding, and had the name of the fraternity house written on her thighs in ball point pen.

At least one of the young men involved in the rape confessed to a friend what had happened. But when the police tried to investigate, the fraternity brothers wouldn't talk. No one would admit they knew anything at all. Soon many of the students started talking about it. They isolated Eleanor and treated her like an outcast. She was made to feel that she invited the attack, that she enjoyed it, and that she was totally to blame. When the lawyers for the young men began to imply that Eleanor was promiscuous and a drunk, she was totally defeated. She quit school, checked into a mental hospital, and tried to kill herself.

Eventually, her date was convicted of felony sexual assault and sentenced to one year and one day in prison. His friends pleaded to lesser charges to lower their punishment.

One of the interesting aspects of this case is that the legal definition of rape depends on whether or not a female consents to have intercourse. Oddly enough, many people believed that Eleanor was guilty because she was drunk. People like this think that if a woman uses alcohol, she is responsible for her own rape. The truth, however, is that if she is too drunk to be able to give her consent, any sexual contact with her is technically a crime. Since most people aren't aware of this, young men often try to use alcohol to force their dates to consent to having sex with them.

"These men robbed me of any pride or hope or self esteem that I had and replaced it with anger, self hate, and fear," says Eleanor. "To see their lives affected is some vindication."

For most young women who are victims of rape, this kind of vindication never comes. Date or acquaintance rape is increasing by leaps and bounds on college campuses around the country. More than 80 percent of all campus rapes involve two people who know each other, and 40 percent of the cases happen in date situations with two people who like each other or who are intimate. The other 40 percent involve more casual acquaintances such as a boyfriend's best friend, a co-worker, a roommate's brother, someone met at a party, a teacher, or someone who lives in the same dorm.

Most dating situations are enjoyable for both males and females and do not end in sexual assault. But date rape, unfortunately, happens more often than most people think.

A female between the ages of 16 and 24 has a good chance of being raped or being the victim of an attempted rape. Among thousands of female college students across the country, one in four is the victim of such an act while she is in college. Yet only five percent ever report what has happened to the police or college authorities.

One of the reasons they don't say anything is that they feel ashamed of what happened to them. Many victims think that maybe it was their fault, and that even if it weren't, no one would believe them. They think it will be less trouble if they keep quiet and don't tell anyone. They hope they will forget in time, and that their feelings of anger and humiliation will go away. Unfortunately, none of these possibilities will come true. It is important to know what are the current myths about rape, and what are the facts. Here is a rundown of myths and facts as compiled by the Orange County, California, Sexual Assault Network:

MYTH: "It could never happen to me."
FACT: Anyone can be a rape victim regardless of age, appearance, ethnic origin, lifestyle, and income level. Reported victims of rape range in age from 1 to 90 years old. One in every three women, and one in every ten men, will be targets of sexual assault. About half of all rapes occur during the day, and the rest during the night.

MYTH: Rape is a nonviolent crime.
FACT: Rape is a violent crime usually committed along with threats of bodily harm or death. Eighty-seven percent of all rapists threaten their victims or carry a weapon. The FBI states that rape *is the most frequently committed violent crime* in the United States today, surpassing murder, robbery and other assaults.

MYTH: The main motive for rape is sexual.
FACT: Men who commit rape need to dominate, humiliate, control, brutalize and have power over another human being. Rape is a sexual expression of aggression, not an aggressive expression of attraction. Two-thirds of rapists could have sex with their wife or another partner if they wanted it.

MYTH: Rapists are *psychotic* or sick men.
FACT: Only three percent of all convicted rapists are diagnosed as clinically psychotic. There is no difference in personality profiles between convicted rapists and other kinds of criminals except that they are not deterred in showing violence toward women. They also believe in strong stereotypes of women's roles. Rapists can be and are doctors, lawyers, police officers, fathers, school teachers, husbands, and the "All-American boy next door."

MYTH: You can only be raped by a stranger. Forced sex with someone you know is not rape.
FACT: Studies show that 60 to 80 percent of all sexual assaults happen when the victim knows her assailant. "Forced sex" is just a misleading term which does not accept the fact that every person has a right to say, "No!" Date rapes are just as devastating—if not more so—than being raped by a stranger because the victim's trust was betrayed. She feels she must be responsible for the attack. These victims will usually not talk to others about what happened, and their trauma goes on longer.

MYTH: Most rapes are interracial.
FACT: The overwhelming majority of rapes involve persons of the same race.

MYTH: Women who are raped are asking for it.
FACT: Women are expected to be attractive in our society, but society blames them if they are too attractive to the wrong person at the wrong time. Rape is not related to the way women dress. Babies in diapers and elderly women have been raped. More than 50 percent of all rapes occur in a woman's own home. A woman at home is hardly asking to be assaulted. When a woman tries to look attractive, she is seeking approval and acceptance, not victimization.

MYTH: All women secretly want to be raped.
FACT: Women do not enjoy attacks, intimidation, injury, abuse, torture, threats, humiliation or degradation. Women fear rape. Rape is where control and power are taken away from the victim. Humiliation, not seduction, is what motivates the rapist.

MYTH: Rape is physically impossible without a woman's consent.
FACT: Anyone can be immobilized by fear or threats of death aimed at either themselves or a loved one. About

87 percent of all rapists use either physical force or some type of weapon to commit the rape. The long lasting emotional injuries of fear, guilt, shame and disgust, added to the physical trauma of possible sexually transmitted diseases, pregnancy or internal injuries, are just some of the emotional problems a woman faces after rape.

MYTH: Rape is over in a few seconds.
FACT: Sexual assaults sometimes last over a period of days. According to the FBI, the average period of time is more than *four hours*. And the victimization does not stop once the rapist frees his victim. Survivors have lost their jobs because of missed time at work, been forced to quit school because of shame, and have turned to drugs or alcohol to deal with their trauma. Most lose their sense of security. It is also estimated that 50 percent of all significant relationships, like marriage, end within six months following the rape as a result of emotional scars and stress.

MYTH: Rape laws are designed to protect women from rape.
FACT: Unfortunately, many rape laws ultimately do more to protect men from the charge of rape. The majority of lawmakers are men in a society that tolerates aggressive sexual behavior. In California, only five percent of all reported rapes end in jail terms because proving the crime is difficult. As a result, the FBI estimates that only one in ten assaults is reported. The actual incarceration rate for rapists is only one-half of one percent. Rape by a spouse is still not a crime in 12 states.

MYTH: There is nothing a woman can do to protect herself against rape without being killed.
FACT: According to a recent study, for every woman who is assaulted, three women manage to fight off their

According to law enforcement agencies, rape is one of the most frequent violent crimes committed in the United States. That is why special rape hotlines and crisis centers are such a necessity in every city and county.

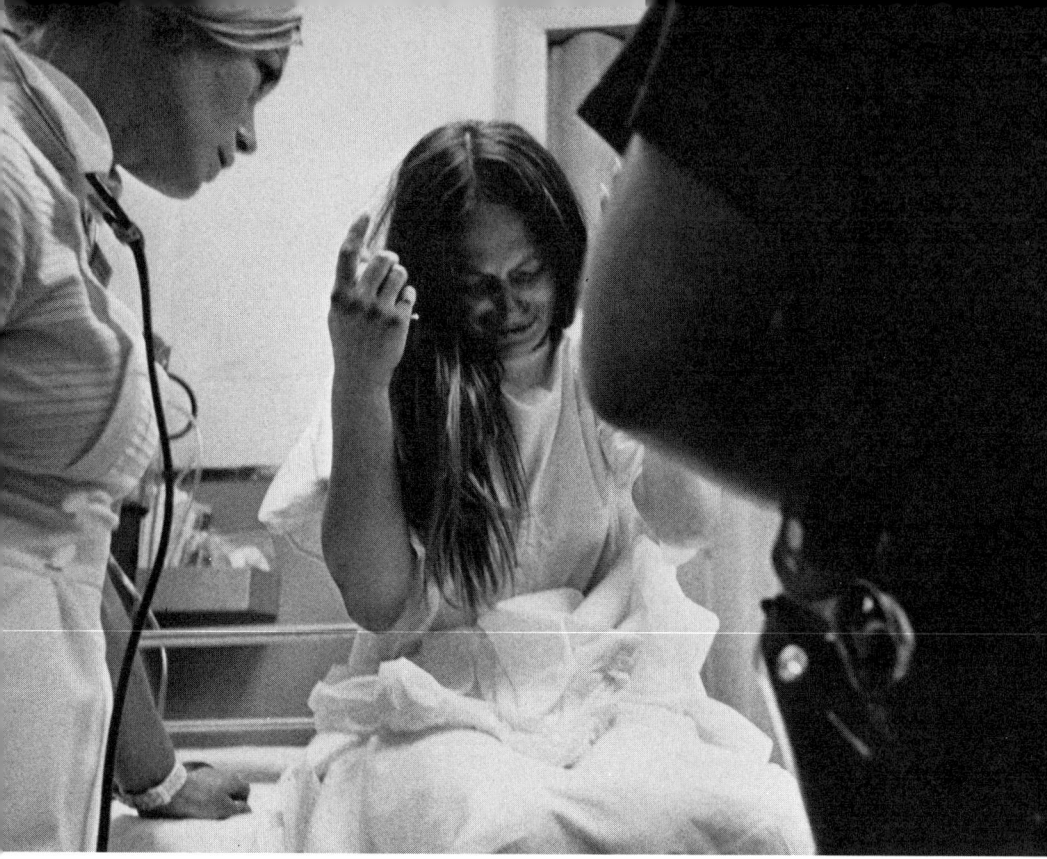

It was once a common attitude that rape was the woman's fault. Now rape victims are medically examined as quickly as possible, and evidence is collected to help convict the rapist.

attackers or slow them down. There are preventive measures women should know to increase their safety. The police state that less than one percent of homicides are associated with rape. Rapists pick vulnerable, unaware victims. They often watch a potential victim ahead of time, so they learn the best time to strike.

When force is used during sex, it changes what is happening from a sexual experience into a violent one. Sex, sexual feelings, and sexual desire are not the motivation for rape. Sex is merely the weapon used to make the victim feel overwhelmed, embarrassed, and powerless—even if the whole encounter began with warm feelings of mutual trust and liking. Once force enters the picture, those feelings change. Fear, anger and confusion are only some of the feelings that replace the warm ones.

    Sadly, anyone can be a rapist. Both males and females have to know when the shift starts to take place—when sex as a warm and mutual event turns into a weapon of force. Males have to know that when a female says "No," she means it. And females must mean what they say. They have to know that it is unfair to play games where sex is concerned to avoid guilt. It is time for members of both sexes to change the cycle of violence that has been a part of most cultures for thousands of years. This can only be done with communication, knowledge, the sharing of feelings, and genuine compassion for others around us.

5 Leaving A Bad Situation

There are many females currently living in bad situations. Some are worse than others. Many women tell themselves that their abusive situation is mild and that there's no need to do anything about it. They are afraid that if they confront the person who is abusing them, it will only make things worse. Unfortunately, they are allowing themselves to be victimized. But the abuse is not their fault.

Changing one's life is not easy. One of the more interesting things about change is that it usually starts small and then grows into something significant. But before talking about what a person can do to change their own situation regarding abuse, it might be helpful to look at that type of situation in a broader context.

If culture is generally based on men being aggressive toward each other and toward women, it stands to reason that aggressive behavior is encouraged. War, for instance, is aggressive. Sports are aggressive. Competition in the workplace is often aggressive. But not all aggression involves physical force. Aggressive behavior is acceptable in certain situations. But not everything can be settled with brute strength.

People learn to be aggressive from their family members and from society in general. For example, if punishment at home is physically violent (spanking, slapping, whipping), children learn that violence is acceptable. Males are often encouraged to be violent because of their gender. They play violent sports and are told that fist fights are "a man's way" of dealing with problems.

If children see that their father is violent with their mother, and if their mother accepts this behavior, then it appears to be a normal way of reacting. And when violence is acceptable in the home, it becomes acceptable outside the home. The United States Department of Justice says that three Americans in 100 are victims of violent crime each year—that works out to six million people each year. And the saddest thing is that the place a person is most likely to be assaulted is in the home, a place that's supposed to offer love and security. Why is so much attention paid to violence in the streets, and so little to violence in the home?

Violence in the streets needs to be controlled because social order is needed for society to function properly. Violence in the streets threatens that order. It is easier to ignore violence in the home, however, and pretend that it affects only those directly involved. But violence in the home can lead to violence elsewhere. If violence at home and on the streets is acceptable, how can we hope to stop solving global problems with violence? Stopping violence means stopping it wherever it occurs—at home, on the streets, and at war.

How can we begin to break this cycle of violent behavior? If a woman is in an abusive family situation, for example, she must get help. It is almost impossible to solve abuse problems all alone. She can find a self-help group, or file a formal complaint. She could request a *restraining order* (a court order that prohibits someone who is harassing you from contacting you). Assault is illegal in the United States, and every U.S. citizen is entitled by law to demand that it stop. An abuser must obey the law, or suffer the consequences. If an abuser sees that there are consequences to violent actions, he or she will no longer feel that they are permitted to use violence as a way of controlling others.

Avoiding Rape

What can someone do to protect against rape? Females should learn some basic self defense. This doesn't mean a black belt in karate; there are other ways of disarming an attacker. Methods of self-protection are taught in schools, police departments and community centers. Instructors also teach verbal ways for dealing with attackers so that no matter how old, small, or weak a woman is, she has a chance of protecting herself.

Learning a self-defense technique can be a matter of life and death. There are many ways a woman can protect herself.

Women should also be aware of some dos and don'ts in helping deal with the crime of rape:
- Women should think about what their rights are in sexual situations. For example, they must know that they can tell anyone—including someone they love or are intimate with—what they will and won't do.
- Women should be careful when dealing with alcohol or illegal drugs. This is especially important, since men often use them as an excuse for abusive behavior.
- A woman must pay attention to the behavior of the men around her. If a man acts more intimate than she wants him to be, gets too close, or doesn't seem to listen to her, her male companion may turn out to be trouble.
- Women should learn to trust their instinctive reactions. Most rape victims say that they felt something wasn't quite right before the attack, but that

they ignored how they felt at the time, and ended up in a dangerous situation. If she feels uncomfortable or isn't sure about the situation, a woman should walk away.

- A woman should not place herself in questionable situations, like going out alone with a man she doesn't know well. And she should definitely not drink too much with people she doesn't know.

Unfortunately, we cannot control other people's actions. It doesn't mean it is a woman's fault if she decides to risk an uncertain situation and is then attacked. A woman can't avoid all dangerous situations, but recognizing as many as possible is important. For instance, maybe it would be wiser to double date the first time she goes out with a new person. Or maybe she should find a friend to jog with her instead of going alone.

Males, too, should take responsibility for their own actions, and be aware of situations that could lead to violence. Some dos and don'ts for males include the following:

- Males should pay attention to what their behavior patterns mean. If they do not think about what it means to control violence, or accept it as a cultural norm, then they stand a good chance of becoming a victim. Not only could they be a victim of ordinary street violence, they are also possible victims of sexual violence as well—it happens to men much more than most people realize.

- Men should consider their own attitudes toward women and sexuality. Men could ask themselves the following questions: Does a woman owe a man something in return for dinner or spending money on her? Has he ever pressured someone to have sex? Does he try to get someone drunk to trick them into sex? Does he see women as equals, or just bodies? What is a man's reaction to pornography?

- Men should think about how the images of women they see affect how they think about them. They should try to understand how their attitudes guide

their behavior around women. They should try to talk about how forced sex impacts women and men, especially if their friends are joking about it.
- Lastly, and most important, men should pay attention when a woman says "no." They should stop what they are doing and try to talk about it. If the woman really means, "yes," she will let a man know. If a man is unsure whether he is getting a "yes" or a "no," then he should stop and ask. And a woman should give him an honest answer. It is a man's responsibility as a friend to make sure his partner is truly consenting.

It is a sad fact that 90 percent of violent crimes are committed by men. If 90 percent of the violent crimes were committed by one particular race or social class, that group would be treated as a very real problem and brought to justice.

Even though women are supposed to be more liberated than they were 20 years ago, the fact remains that women are still afraid to walk in the streets at night. They are still being abused in their homes. Clearly, the women's liberation movement has not achieved all it hoped to. Part of the problem is that not enough women speak out and demand that their status be improved. There is still more work to be done. By remaining silent, women give the message that they are willing to remain victims.

Victims Of Rape

If you or someone you know has been raped, there are important things you should know. Survivors of rape suffer a great deal of physical and emotional trauma during the rape, and this trauma continues for a very long period of time afterward. The first thing a victim should do is try to understand the trauma. If victims of rape are treated with sensitivity and understanding, there will be less tendency for future victims to remain silent about what has happened to them.

Both males and females can act in responsible ways to help prevent rape.

There are two phases in the rape trauma syndrome:

1. *The acute phase*, where the victim's life is totally disrupted by the crime. During the acute phase, the victim fears injury, mutilation and death—no doubt in reaction to being threatened and violated. Some victims are able to express their emotions, and some are very controlled. The expressive ones show anger, fear and anxiety, but the controlled ones show an outward calm, composed attitude. They are all prone to mood swings, emotional outbursts, and experience feelings of degradation, humiliation, shame, guilt, self-blame, and desire for revenge. Although they try to block thoughts of the attack, they keep popping up.

This phase lasts from ten days to one month and includes physical reactions. A rape victim may feel sore all over, have trouble sleeping, and even scream in her sleep from nightmares. They lose their appetite, complain of stomach problems, and say that food doesn't taste right.

2. The *long-term phase*, during which the survivor tries to rebuild her disrupted life. This second phase can last one year or more. It is during this time that the victim tries to cope with what happened to her and reorganize her life so she can deal with her fear and with men. Many accomplish this by changing where they live, changing their jobs, and their lifestyles. Some continue to go to school or work, but refuse to participate in social activities. A continuing problem during the second phase is recurring dreams or nightmares. The nightmares are of two different types: a) The victim finds herself back in the situation where the rape occurred. She tries to get herself out of it, but fails. b) The victim sees herself committing acts of violence against other people (occurs later during the second phase).

Survivors also develop *phobias*—fear of specific things, like the smell of tobacco, gasoline, or alcohol, if these were part of the rape. They also may fear men, or have a diminished sex drive. Some victims have a silent reaction to rape, where they show all the symptoms, but never mention that a rape occurred.

Eventually, the victim may reach a level where she is again comfortable with herself, her surroundings, and the men in her life. Some women never reach this level of comfort. Rape disrupts the life of the survivor in four areas: physical, emotional, sexual and social. Victims need and should receive immediate support and counseling.

The first thing you should do if someone you know tells you they have been raped is listen. Ask questions if you don't understand something, but don't ask for specific details. There may be gaps in her story, but be patient and let her continue at her own pace. Something similar may have happened in your life. If so, mention it briefly, but don't go on and on about your own problem.

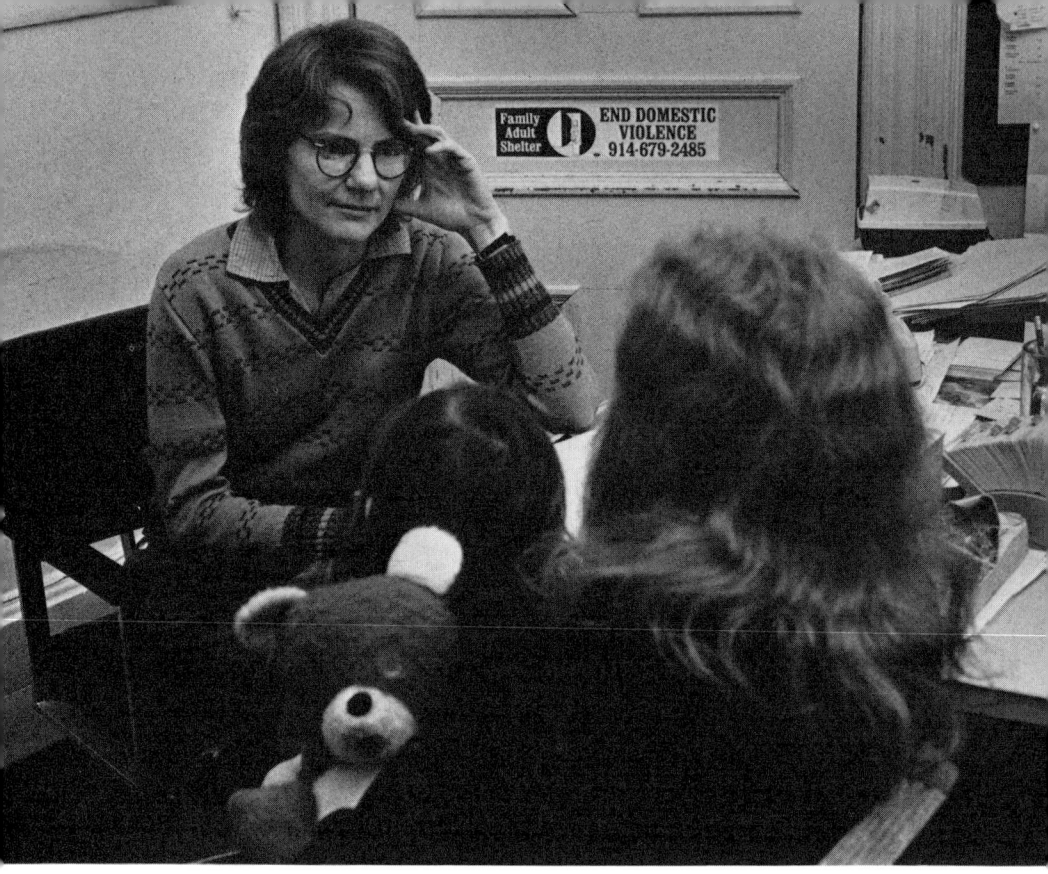

Counseling is an important part of the recovery process when women are victims of rape or domestic violence.

Second, be supportive. Tell her you care about her and how she is feeling. Ask how she is feeling emotionally, or how she is dealing with what happened, but don't insist that she give you information about which she seems to be uncomfortable. Tell her that what she is feeling is normal and understandable (anger, fear, guilt, embarrassment). Try to get her professional help and some supportive people she can see and talk to. Don't be critical, and don't make decisions for her such as notifying the police. This should be her decision.

Recognize that she has emotional and medical problems that should be dealt with immediately and professionally. Talk to her about the emotional concerns, such as how this is having an impact on her life, her relationships, and her behavior. Talk to her about the medical concerns. After all, she might have sustained real trauma internally such as cuts, bruises, vaginal damage, pregnancy, infection, or venereal disease. The sooner they are recognized, the sooner they can be taken care of.

Lastly, help her find some kind of community services that can help. Support groups, for example, can provide a setting where she can come to terms with what has happened. Very often, professional help is necessary for a woman to fully regain her self-esteem, trust, and the life she led before the attack.

6 A Woman's Rights

Both assault and rape are illegal. If you report a rape or an assault, it can be prosecuted—but only if you press charges. A victim has the right to take legal action against an assailant. Unfortunately, sometimes people must demand and continue to demand that their rights be upheld.

There are now many more services for women than there were 20 or 30 years ago. The women's movement has made it easier for women to take legal action against assailants. It has also encouraged the creation of support groups and professional services for victims of rape and abuse. Rape hotlines and crisis intervention services are available in many communities that can help a victim who does not know where to go for help. There has also been a great increase in available shelters for battered women. These shelters have counselors and other support services for those who wish to break away from an abusive relationship, to press charges, or obtain financial support.

There are certain rights of which a woman should be aware. Knowing your basic human rights will give you the strength to get out of a bad situation. For example, you have a right to express your opinions, see your friends, and express your emotional, sexual, and intellectual needs. You have the right to get professional help for yourself or for your relationship when you need it. You have the right to be free from physical attack. You have the right to end any relationship. Know your rights and insist upon having them upheld.

Studies have shown that when an abusive partner is arrested and charged, it can have a deterrent effect on the abuser. But if a woman does not press charges, it allows her partner to think his abusive behavior is acceptable. He usually returns and resumes the abuse. Sometimes it is even worse. If she fears that her life or the lives of her children will be at risk if she files a formal complaint, then she should definitely get

It may be difficult for a woman to press charges against someone who has raped or assaulted her, but it may keep the assailant from attacking someone else.

out—fast. That is the time to seek safety in a shelter for abused women.

Just 20 years ago there were only eight shelters for battered women in the United States. Now there are over 1,000. In these shelters women and children are given food, clothing, and a safe place to stay. Counselors are available to help them get a new start in life, and their whereabouts are kept secret from their abusive partner. Abused women are told that they do have a choice in how they will live.

It is far better to leave or report the abuser than it is to try to deal with the violence. Because of cases brought before the courts by battered women, changes have been made in the way these kinds of cases have been decided.

An example of such a case involves a woman named Tracy Thurman. She was awarded $2.3 million in a suit against 24 police officers in Connecticut. She had repeatedly called the police department when her husband attacked her, but the police never provided her with the protection she needed.

When the last of her husband's attacks occurred, she called the police. But by the time they arrived 25 minutes later, she had been stabbed 13 times and kicked in the head. Even after the police arrived, her husband continued to wander around the yard, screaming and cursing. Then he went inside the house, grabbed their little son, and dropped him on his mother's bleeding body. He kicked her in the head once again before he was finally arrested. Her suit charged that the police had acted negligently in protecting her and her son from harm. Today, even though Tracy Thurman was awarded a lot of money, she is permanently scarred and partially paralyzed from that final attack.

Cases like this have prompted the United States Attorney General's Task Force on Family Violence to recommend that family violence be recognized and responded to as a criminal activity. If batterers are treated as common criminals, they will stop their abusive behavior much more readily. Assault is assault, and against the law, no matter what the relationship between people is.

If You Need Help

If you or a family member or friend needs help, you can check your local phone directory yellow pages for services listed under "Battered Persons' Aid," or "Crisis Intervention Service." Or you can call the National Coalition Against Domestic Violence, where someone will recommend a local service in your area.

If you need help in a rape case, call your local hospital or police department or go directly to a hospital emergency room or police station. You can also

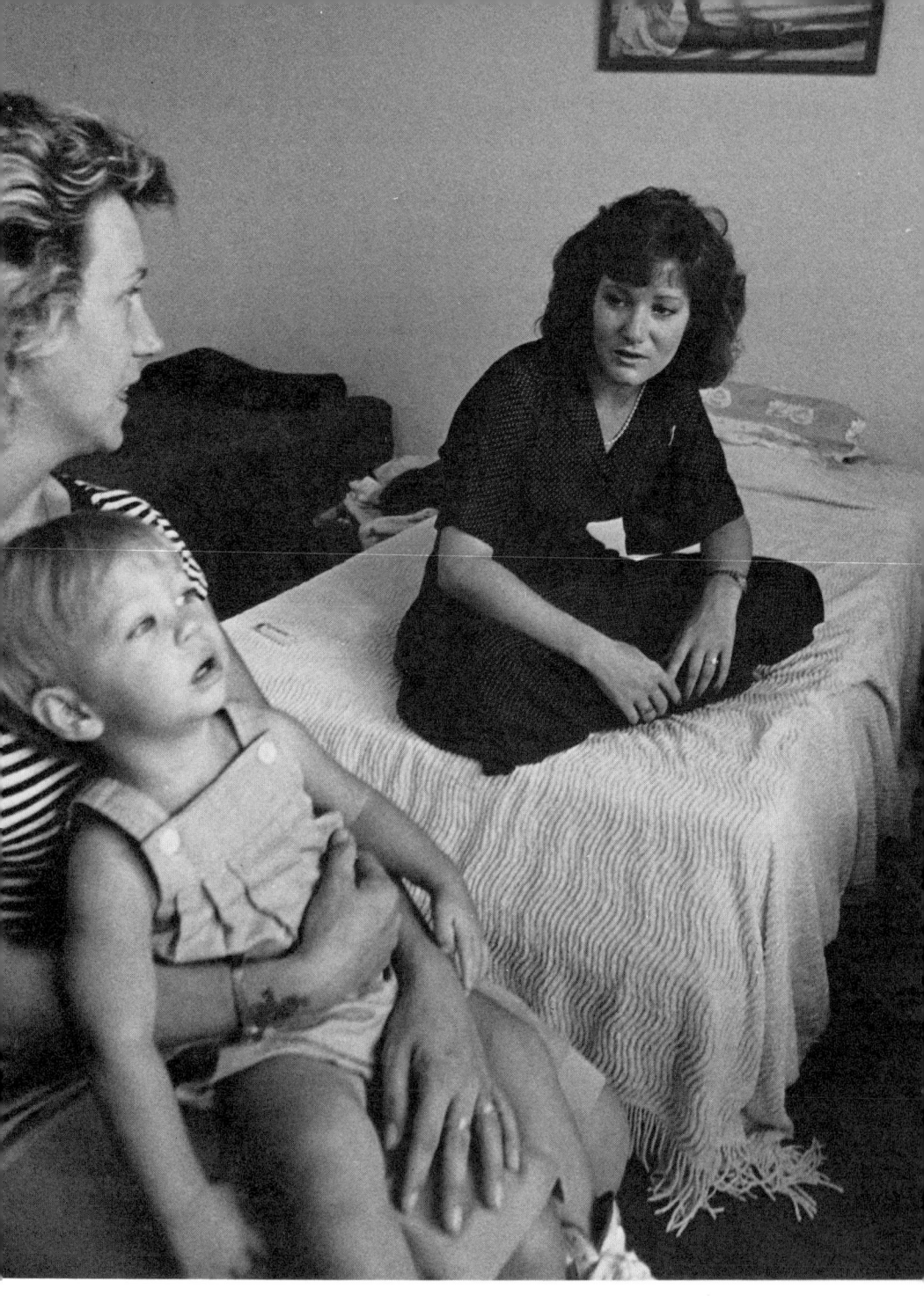
Many shelters protect both a woman and her children from an abusive husband or father.

check with other human service agencies such as Child Guidance, Child Protective Services, or the local YWCA. They are aware of rape crisis services in your area. You can also contact one of the national organizations listed below. If you need to talk with someone immediately, call 411 for information and get a telephone number for these organizations.

National Center for the Prevention and Control of Rape
Room 15-99, Parklawn Bldg.
5600 Fishers Lane
Rockville, Maryland 20857

National Coalition Against Sexual Assault
P.O. Box 7156
Austin Texas, 78712

National Board YWCA of the U.S.A.
600 Lexington Avenue
New York, N.Y. 10022

    More and more women are speaking out about date and acquaintance rape. At Brown University, one woman started the process of speaking out by using one of the bathrooms. She wrote on the wall, "[Name deleted] is a rapist." In a few days, more and more names were added of other male students. Even though janitors kept washing the list off the walls, it kept returning, with more and more names, and suggestions as well. Male students started sneaking into the bathroom to see if their names were on the list.
    Soon, other lists started in other bathrooms. Here are some quotes: "Let's start naming names. If we don't take care of each other, no one will." "Keep this list going strong. Warn others. Do not be afraid!" "How can I not be afraid? The man who assaulted me thinks I'm the one who wrote his name on the list. It must have been a different woman he assaulted."

Mutual respect for another person—and accepting their right to be free from violence—is a must in the building of any lasting, loving relationship.

Speaking out and naming names. Victims know, as all of us should, that if we don't start to protect ourselves, no one else will.

There are lots of things you can do to help improve the lives of the battered woman. You can volunteer to work on hotlines. You can find your local rape crisis centers or shelters and help them raise money. But most important, you can fight abuse and victimization by demanding that everyone around you treat you with the love, respect and admiration that you truly deserve.

Glossary

ABUSE. Harmful and unreasonable treatment by word or deed.

ALCOHOL ABUSE. Drinking alcoholic beverages to excess so that the alcohol has a negative effect on the behavior of the abuser, his or her effectiveness on the job, and the well-being of the family.

ASSAULT. A violent attack, either physical or verbal. The threat to use force upon another person, then carrying it out.

BATTERING. The unlawful beating of another person.

DATE RAPE. Rape that occurs between acquaintances on a date.

DOMESTIC. Having to do with the family or the home.

DRUG ABUSE. Using illegal drugs.

EXTENDED FAMILIES. A household with parents, one or more children, grandparents, and sometimes other relatives.

MOLESTATION. Physical assault that generally involves sexual contact of some type.

PHOBIA. A persistent, illogical, abnormal, or intense fear.

PSYCHOTIC. Having a mental disorder.

RAPE. Forced sexual contact.

RAPE TRAUMA SYNDROME. The psychological effects on a woman after she has been raped. The *acute phase* can last up to a month, where the victim's life is completely disrupted, and when emotional outbursts are most common. The *long-term phase* can last up to a year, where the victim makes many changes in their lifestyle to get their lives back in order.

RESTRAINING ORDER. When the courts issue an order requiring that a person stay outside of a certain distance from another person, their home, school, or place of work. Violating the order risks prosecution.

SEXUAL ABUSE. Any forced, violent molestation of another person that includes sexual contact.

SEXUAL HARASSMENT. When a person is threatened with loss of job or status unless they provide sexual favors. Also the continuous and inappropriate mention of sexual acts in a job or school situation.

TABOO. Something forbidden or frowned upon; until recent years, openly discussing sexual abuse and rape was discouraged.

Bibliography

Bradshaw, John. *On Healing The Shame That Binds You.* Health Communications, 1988.

The Family. Health Communications, 1988.

Cantrell, Leslie. *Into The Light: A Guide For Battered Women.* The Charles Franklin Press, 1986.

Gelles, Richard & Murray A. Strauss. *Intimate Violence: The Definitive Study Of The Causes And Consequences Of Abuse In The American Family.* Simon & Schuster, 1988.

McEvoy, Alan W. and Jeff B. Brookings. *If She Is Raped: A Book For Husbands, Fathers, And Male Friends.* Learning Publications, 1984.

Stanko, Elizabeth A. *Intimate Intrusions: Women's Experience Of Male Violence.* Routledge & Kegan Paul, 1985.

White, Evelyn C. *Chain, Chain Change: For Black Women Dealing With Physical and Emotional Abuse.* The Seal Press, 1985.

Index

abuse
　child, 24-27
　defined, 23
　getting help, 55
　myths about, 27-31
　physical, 25
　reporting, 54-55
　sexual, 25
alcohol abuse, 28 *see also* abuse

date rape *see* rape
domestic violence, 10-11, 20, 29
drug abuse, 28 *see also* abuse

emotional neglect, 24
extended families, 20

men
　abusive husbands, 18
　and authority, 18
　attitude toward sex, 46-47

molestation, 25

phobia(s), 49

rape
　and alcohol, 33, 34
　and feelings of shame, 35-36, 48
　and use of violence, 36, 38
　case studies, 15, 33-34
　date rape, 7, 10, 33-34, 37, 55-59
　defined, 10, 15, 34
　frequency of, 10, 34-35
　how to help a victim, 49-51
　laws, 38
　motives, 36, 40-41
　myths about, 36-40
　preventing, 40, 44-47
　profile of rapist, 16, 36
　victims of, 47-51
rape trauma syndrome
　acute phase, 48-49
　long-term phase, 49
restraining order, 44

sexual abuse, 7-8, 25 *see also* abuse
sexual harassment, 8

violence *see also* domestic violence,
　rape
　acceptability of, 18-20
　committed by men, 47
　in history, 11-13
　in society, 43-44
　reasons it occurs, 18, 20-21
　shelters for battered women,
　　55-57
　victim as the "cause," 29

women's movement, women's
　rights, 13, 18, 47, 53-59

About The Author

Leslie McGuire is a graduate of Barnard College and has been writing books for young people for 15 years. She was contributing editor to the Concise Columbia Encyclopedia, as well as the author of biographies of Napoleon, Catherine the Great, and Anastasia. McGuire has written over 160 books for children and young adults. She is presently living in Southern California.

Picture Credits

AP Wide World Photos: 26, 45
The Image Works: 12 (Carl Glassman); 39 (Rhoda Sidney); 42, 50, 52 (Mark Antman); 45 (Alan Carey); 54 (Gatewood); 56 (Bob Daemmrich)
Nancy Durrell McKenna: 14 (from *Woman's Experience of Sex* by Sheila Kitzinger, published by Dorling Kindersley UK 1983/Photo Researchers, Inc.
Photo Researchers, Inc.: 4 (Andy Levin); 6 (Will & Deni McIntyre); 9 (Arthur Tress); 17 (Barbara Rios); 19 (Stan Levy); 22 (Susan Oristaglio); 30 (Bettye Lane); 32, 40 (Robert Goldstein); 35 (David M. Grossman); 48 (Richard Hutchings); 58 (Spencer Grant)